Inside the Horse's Eye

poems by

Patsy Kisner

Finishing Line Press
Georgetown, Kentucky

Inside the Horse's Eye

ACKNOWLEDGMENTS

Grateful acknowledgments to the following journals and anthology where these
poems first appeared, some in slightly different versions:

Forge: The Mouse
Frogpond: Cutting Open
Modern Haiku: New Barn Completed
Spoon River Poetry Review: The Old House
The Tower Journal: Doubts, In the Hush
The Red Moon Anthology: Cutting Open

Publisher: Leah Maines

Editor: Christen Kincaid

Cover Art: Stanzi/Shutterstock.com

Author Photo: Patricia Haught, 2Haught Photography

Cover Design: Elizabeth Maines

Printed in the USA on acid-free paper.
Order online: www.finishinglinepress.com
              also available on amazon.com

Author inquiries and mail orders:
Finishing Line Press
P. O. Box 1626
Georgetown, Kentucky 40324
U. S. A.

Table of Contents

"I will lift up mine eyes unto the hills."

Psalm 121:1

WRINKLES

Wrinkles reflect
back when
I look—
like small furrows
on the scalp
of mother earth,
fallow ground
that has been plowed
and now waits
to feel
what grows.

THE OLD HOUSE

The old house
lies in a heap.
They left everything
of his inside
for trespassers
to ramble by
and see.
Even his coat
hangs on the parlor wall
with a bird nest
in the pocket.

GHOSTS

I got so angry
at that generation—
I disowned many
for their hurtful words,
but I can't escape
the fact that I
came from them.
I can't detach from their DNA,
thus I'm forced
to look their ghosts
straight in the eye,
find the ugly
and pluck it out.

THE MURDER OF JAMES STURM, 1886

Red dripped
like paint slung
against a
wall—
his life,
his dreams
falling
in crimson
beads
while the night
birds flew
away.

THE WHIPPOORWILL

See the whippoorwill
with large, round
night eyes.
Do they shine
so she can
sing?

COME ENJOY THE DAY

Come enjoy the day,
they said,
but I had picked buckets
of beans—
long, smooth and green.
And while everyone
laughed, talked about this
and admired that,
all I could do
was think about
canning the beans.

MY HOUSE

Though you are
made of wood,
I know you move—
that atoms shift
about and pulse.
I hear the beat,
feel vibrations
when I'm still.
You wrap me
in your living
though people
say you're dead.

DOUBTS

Doubts creep in
to cover dreams with mold,
but ugly only grows
in unkempt spaces,
so I scrub the floors
and wipe the walls clean
before the spore
can grow.

SIXTEEN DEGREES

I tend the
farm as rushed
as snow and
ice allow,
all the while
the rhododendrons
sigh as winter
wilts their
leaves.

IN THE HUSH

In the hush
of the brush
the deer
lies within.
Watch her
eyes blink.

MARCH

March roars in
with snow and ice
while a bullfrog
lies smashed
along the road.

NEW BARN COMPLETED

New barn completed—
somewhere a sawed stump
with a hundred rings.

CUTTING OPEN

Cutting open
a bale of hay—
the smell of summer.

GRAIN BUCKETS

Grain buckets rattle—
eating fills the barn
with life.

INSIDE THE HORSE'S EYE

Inside the horse's eye
I see
me.

MOUNTAIN WOMAN

There's a mountain woman in me.
She broods over my discontent
with modern things,
lures me with traditions
and her calm, simple ways.
Yes, there's a mountain woman in me,
has been from the start.
I am the seed that
has evolved into her.
She's in my mirror
when I look.

IF I REMINISCE

If I reminisce,
I'll choose
the now—
see that bird
flutter red feathers
among the rhododendron
and dew drip off
the wisteria leaf,
all the while
fog lifts
from the
hollow—watch
it gently go,
twisting ever so
slightly as it
moves.

IN THIS PICTURE

In this picture
your gold hair
falls around
your shoulders—
living, growing.
Now I cling
to one precious
lock.
It is all
I have of
the physical you—
the one that
could softly
lean against
my shoulder.

FADED

I faded
when you
died—hid
beneath the
rim of holy water
to separate
myself
from life,
yet there it
was—causing
ripples to
brush against
my skin.

I SAW AN OWL

I saw an owl
in daylight
with feathers
brown and black—
his eyes
too piercing
for the sun.

THE MOUSE

The mouse
gnaws within
the walls,
nuisance knowing
not—and
thus the trap
is set.

THE ONE

You had to
be the one—
all because of
the way
your words
fell into the
cup of my
outstretched
hand.

I CANCELLED WORK TODAY

I cancelled work today—
feigned illness.
In truth there was
sickness of the heart
longing to cocoon itself,
yet the number of layers
will never matter.
Some worm will gnaw a hole
big enough to peek through,
big enough for light
to penetrate from a sun that
will surely rise—after
the setting of the moon.

JACK-IN-THE-PULPIT

See the jack-in-
the-pulpit—
that pitcher of
hope with the
lid half
open.

BEHIND THE EYE

Behind the eye
every second
lingers—
hides in the folds
of a complex brain.
Would you dare
remember every
one?

LOOK UP

Look up and
feast upon the
star—the one
I always see,
here in my
home of thirty
years. I
sit and watch
as it never
leaves.

Patsy Kisner lives in rural West Virginia in an area where her family has lived for five generations. A graduate of Glenville State College in Glenville, WV, she worked in the Calhoun County School System for fifteen years. She and her husband, Phillip, are the parents of two daughters, Mary, now deceased, and Maria, who lives nearby.

www.ingramcontent.com/pod-product-compliance
Lightning Source LLC
LaVergne TN
LVHW041329080426
835513LV00008B/652